JOSEPH BEUYS was born in 19 Conscripted into the army, he suff plane crashes. After a period in an English p end of the War, he began to study natural science, but disillusioned with its basic tenets he switched to art. From 1947 to 1951 he studied at the Düsseldorf Art Academy with the sculptor Edward Mataré. At that time he encountered Rudolf Steiner's work. After years of struggling as an artist and times of deep depression, in 1961 Beuys became Professor of Monumental Sculpture at the Düsseldorf Academy, from which he was expelled in 1972 for challenging the quota system by taking on all students who wanted to learn. During this period he worked with groups like Fluxus whose experimental, interventionist 'events' had much in common with his own strategies and concerns. This led, from 1965, to Fluxus-festivals and 'happenings', and life-long collaborations with artists like Nam June Paik.

Following his first gallery 'action' (a term he coined) in 1965, 'Teaching Paintings to a Dead Hare', Beuys' international reputation grew. He became known for his largely silent actions with substances, creatures and instruments of all kinds, and provocative formulations like 'Every Human being is an Artist' and 'Art=Capital'. He participated in many major international events, including the Venice Biennale, Edinburgh Festival and five Documenta exhibitions from 1964. In 1979 he was honoured with a major retrospective at the Guggenheim Museum, New York. In the 1980s there were more exhibitions of Beuys' work than of any other artist, and his influence on younger generations of artists has been extensive.

Beuys – alchemist, social visionary and artist – died in

1986, just after receiving the prestigious Lehmbruck Prize. He left behind him not only numerous large-scale installations and site-works, hundreds of provocative multiples and small objects, thousands of drawings (many on blackboards developed as part of 'permanent conference' / dialogue actions), documented social sculpture forums about energy, new money forms and direct democracy, but above all a methodology, 'theory of sculpture', and ideas like 'parallel process' and 'social sculpture'. These ideas – underlying his major social process works such as 'Organisation for Direct Democracy', '7000 Oaks', the 'Free International University' and the 'Honey Pump at the Workplace' – contain unexplored seeds and are a profound basis for new generations of ecological, social process and interdisciplinary practitioners.

WHAT IS MONEY?

A discussion

JOSEPH BEUYS

with Johann Philipp von Bethmann,
Hans Binswanger, Werner Ehrlicher and
Rainer Willert

Afterword by Ulrich Rösch

CLAIRVIEW

Clairview Books
Hillside House, The Square
Forest Row, RH18 5ES

www.clairviewbooks.com

Published by Clairview 2010

Originally published in German under the title *Was ist Geld?, Eine Podiumsdiskussion* by FIU-Verlag, Wangen, in 1991. This edition is based on the second edition, 2009

Translated from German by Isabelle Boccon-Gibod. Translation revised and edited by Clairview Books

© FIU-Verlag, Wangen 2009
This translation © Clairview Books Ltd. 2010

Picture credits: p. 8–9, Südwestpresse, 1.12.88 (photo, S. Resch); p. 26, from catalogue 'Luna Luna', Munich 1987; front cover, pp. 33, 42, 85, 87, Hallen für neue Kunst, Schaffhausen (from Mario Kamer, *Joseph Beuys, Das Kapital Raum 1970–1977*, Heidelberg 1991); p. 54, Achberger Beuys-Archiv, FIU Verlag/Rainer Rappmann

A catalogue record for this book is available from the British Library

ISBN 978 1 905570 25 6

Cover by Andrew Morgan Design incorporating a blackboard drawing by Joseph Beuys
Typeset by DP Photosetting, Neath, West Glamorgan
Printed and bound by Gutenberg Press, Malta

Contents

Foreword

Over twenty-five years have passed since this debate took place in Ulm, so it is legitimate to ask why we feel it is still relevant: in what way does it continue to illumine our current economic situation?

While much has changed in the intervening period, some things decidedly have not. Our world is still dominated by a concept of money and capital that makes money into a commodity, the continual object of power struggles and even wars, and a means whereby human labour is degraded into a tradable commodity. Ultimately this outlook is destroying our social and ecological fabric.

Since the western economic system, the 'social market economy', triumphed globally, it has been generally regarded as the only viable system, obviating the need to search for other, better approaches.

Yet today – for instance in ecology – we really only treat symptoms rather than causes. Critical potential in our society seems often to have been submerged, frustrated or even paralysed. Underlying causes are not really perceived, let alone discussed. Without proper (that is, appropriate and responsive) insight into a problem, without perceiving what is at work in it, we cannot expect to find remedies. This is true of all fields of endeavour, and especially of money.

The debate published here is the only recorded instance in which Beuys took up the core idea of a transformation of our view of money and capital, and engaged with other views on the subject. It becomes evident 'that in these competing opinions, Joseph Beuys's unorthodox views are more than able to hold their own'* as the press reported at the time. The debate is marked by lively and on occasion humorous exchanges.

From the 1970s onwards, Beuys increasingly focused on a new concept of capital and money, drawing essentially on the findings of Wilhelm Schmundt, a student of Rudolf Steiner. In an appendix to the present edition, Ulrich Rösch has compiled and summarized these ideas to help the reader gain better acquaintance with them. In all his work, Beuys was concerned with nothing less than elaborating a 'view of art that can solve the problem of capital'.† Right up to his death, he pursued this path unerringly, with the means at his disposal and at the most diverse levels, as recorded for instance in the many board drawings created during the 100 days of the 1977 documenta6 event, in connection with the 'Honey Pump in the Workplace' installation. This, in turn, flowed into 'The Capital Space 1970–1977', from which the board drawings in this volume are taken, and which is now housed permanently at the 'Hallen für neue Kunst' ['New Art Galleries'] in Schaffhausen, Germany. It was this work that gave Rainer Willert the idea of inviting Joseph Beuys to participate in the debate in Ulm.

Here we see Beuys as always pushing at the boundaries of traditions in art which might seek to confine him. In this

---

* *Schwäbische Zeitung*, Ulm edition, 1.12.1984: 'Beuys und die Ökonome: Ein-Mann-Show mit drei Statisten' ['Beuys and the economists: one-man show with three extras'].
† J. Beuys/M. Ende: *Kunst und Politik – Ein Gespräch* ['Art and Politics – a Conversation'].

debate he confronts not only visitors to art galleries but each and every one of us with the unsolved problem of money.

The current economic crisis has highlighted the destructive ways in which we use and abuse our most precious assets: our innate capacities and creativity. We are still caught in the trap of 'working to earn'. Yet we do not in reality merely work to be 'remunerated', but rather to produce goods and services that serve others, that others need.

We still do not properly differentiate what money is: not a commodity and thus a tradable asset, but a means to facilitate economic processes. Beuys's culminating statement — that 'art = capital' — has been generally misunderstood. Today we suddenly find ourselves in a position where we can ask, again, whether Beuys's thinking might offer a real solution for the problems that so sorely beset us.

Michaela Meyer
Rainer E. Rappmann

'What is Money?': a discussion held on 29 November 1984 at The Meeting House in Ulm, Germany

Introducing the participants

Joseph BEUYS (1921–1986):
Most significant German artist of the 20th century, Professor of Monumental Sculpture at the Düsseldorf Arts Academy, he developed the 'enlarged concept of art' (the discipline of 'Social Sculpture' as art), a concept suggesting that everyone can and should explore the laws of the social organism and engage in the shaping of it.

Johann Phlipp von BETHMANN (1924–2007):
Former banker, co-owner of the Bethmann Brothers bank, author of various publications including: *Die Zinskatastrophe* ['The Catastrophe of Interest'] (1982), member of various boards of directors and supervisory boards.

Hans Christoph BINSWANGER (b. 1929):
Professor Emeritus of Political Economics and former director of the Research Society for Political Economics at St. Gall College, recipient of the German federal award for environmental protection (1980), author of various publications, including *Geld v. Magie* ['Money and Magic – An Economist Reads Goethe's Faust'] (1985) as well as *Geld u. Natur* ['Money and Nature – Economic Growth between Economy and Ecology'] (1991).

Werner EHRLICHER (b. 1920):
Professor Emeritus of Financial Sciences at Freiburg University; former director of the Institute for Savings, Deposit and Credit, author of various publications, including *Geld- u. Währungspolitik in der BRD* ['Money and Monetary Policy in the BRD'], 1982 (published for the 25th anniversary of the German Federal Bank) and *Der volkswirtsch Sparprozess* ['Savings in Political Economics'] (1985).

Rainer WILLERT (b. 1947):
Studied economics. He organized and chaired the discussion published here and later worked in the field of developmental aid in Paraguay.

Rainer Willert's initiative and the motivation that led to the debate are highlighted in the following passage from a long letter which Willert wrote to the publishers in 1991, seven years after the discussion took place:

> I studied economics and had thus become a 'money man' before I really started trying to see what money is. Although this question is intrinsic to the profession, no really satisfactory answer was forthcoming ... As Ehrlicher rightly said during the debate, economists have solved the problem by offering functional definitions. Accordingly, money is everything that fulfils three functions: a means of payment, a means of storing value, and a unit of calculation. In the history of economics this was not always so. In recent centuries people reflected comprehensively on the nature of money, but have not done so any more for well over a hundred years.

After finishing my studies I kept pondering this question – the nature of money, not just how to lay one's hands on it. And at the same time, since the narrower discipline of economics no longer engaged with this in a broader sense, I looked around to see what the views of other disciplines might be.

I only became aware that artists could address this question when an exhibition was held at Dusseldorf Kunsthalle (art gallery) in 1978 entitled 'Museum of Money'. It included works by Beuys ... But it wasn't until I saw the exhibition 'Quartetto' in Venice in 1984 that I was moved to question Beuys in more detail about the theme. The exhibition included blackboards with texts describing economic and monetary circulation streams. To an economist's eye there was something very familiar here and yet, it seemed, more than was fully explained or easily explicable. The same year I saw 'The Capital Space' installation in Schaffhausen, but still did not grasp Beuys's theory of money, value and economics. His documenta installations – '7000 Oaks Trees' in 1982, and the 'Honey Pump at the Workplace' in 1977 – seemed to show, however, that he was engaging with these issues in an original way.

In retrospect, what happened fairly randomly and haphazardly was that Beuys's insights and my own developing understanding came together without this being immediately apparent. In 1984, when I considered the theme of money again for a college course in Ulm, it occurred to me that Beuys would certainly have something to say on the subject. At the same time it seemed to me that the art world could not properly respond to his initiatives: it simply has too little understanding of these issues and the context in which they're embedded. Or, still worse, art is compelled to live in its ghetto. On the other hand I had repeatedly spoken to bankers with an artistic inclination about Beuys

as an economic theorist. Some of them grew very impatient at the mention of his name: 'We're money professionals, an artist is something quite different ...'

Thus the art world does not have the tools to grasp

From left to right: Werner Ehrlicher, Hans Christoph Binswanger, Rainer Willert, Joseph Beuys, Johann Philipp Freiherr von Bethmann

Beuys's social impetus, and artistically inclined economists, for their part, insist on leaving Beuys where (they
believe) he belongs — in newspapers' 'culture' sections.

For the discussion in Ulm I decided not to have anyone
from the art and culture world alongside Beuys. Instead I
would have people who knew something about economics,
solid professionals who would also be unabashed about
contradicting the 'guru'. Ehrlicher fitted the bill. Binswanger, I hoped, with his ecological perspective, but also an
economist, would act as an intermediary between them,
and could summarize and evaluate. Von Bethmann, a
renegade economist, was to demonstrate that things can't
go on as they are.

I do believe this all worked rather well, though I have to
admit that I was not suddenly struck by illumination during the debate. Only after many repeated re-hearings, and
re-readings of the transcript, does it seem to me that my
understanding has advanced a little.

WILLERT: Good evening, a warm welcome to you all. I'd like to offer a brief, prepared introduction. It is very short — and then we'll go straight into the discussion.

So please imagine that here, in this space, an artist has turned the chairs by 180° and calls this a 'correction'. No doubt this correction would get us closer to a truth, since the audience would then be facing the way that corresponds to this church's architecture and original intent. So, you are all looking in the wrong direction. This metaphor brings us directly to our subject: money — a theme that is very likely not the reason most of you came here tonight. But let's still ask: '*What is money?*' 'Nothing': that's the only possible answer. But it works. Money works because in our heads, yes, we don't think of it as nothing. And because entire networks of institutions — here I'll mention only banks and the pricing system — emerged from this same falsehood and established themselves on its basis, making it their business to hide this nothingness from view.

So, money works. And its most important work is to secure its future: in other words, to make sure we go on desiring it in future too. In light fiction, at least, an intriguing character is one who doesn't show his hand straight away. This brings to mind the acrobat's act on the high wire. Money is desirable when it reveals only a portion of its powers, and in doing so excites the imagination. The theoretical knowledge that you can buy something with money feeds the imagination — so much so that you don't really need to buy anything. This would be fine were it not for the sceptic, who only believes what he sees before him. Simply put, *interest* was created for him. So, interest was created to help the sceptic, so that he could always see bank statements reflecting his money's worth in nice black numbers. But since those who perform this demonstration – the bankers – are no charlatans, they undertake to truly earn the interest. They do so by lending, and thus debt grows exponentially. The debts of borrowers grow. In other words, someone who borrows money from the bank has debt. The bank on the other hand owes to the first individual who deposited his money, who starts owing to himself by spending his money.

Well, that's my introduction, and no doubt it's high time to correct it in various ways. Mr Ehrlicher, would you be so kind?

EHRLICHER: Well, there is no general answer to a question such as 'What is money', if this is the question we ask, because all through history money has never ceased to evolve. And the question can't be answered in a general way because money, like everything, can be approached with very different motives.

We could perhaps approach the subject from a more general perspective by first asking what motivations we may have when we try to get near an entity of this sort, a human creation, and therefore a cultural phenomenon. Here, Max Sheler[*] established a distinction which I have always perceived as very helpful, where he differentiates between three

---

[*] Max Scheler (1874–1928), philosopher, professor in Cologne.

types of knowledge: knowledge for the sake of achievement, knowledge for the sake of education, and knowledge for the purpose of redemption. Perhaps it will be helpful, and at the outset allow us to categorize answers to this general question – of which you'll certainly hear a great variety this evening – to consider for a moment the issues which present themselves when we strive for these diverse forms of knowledge about an entity which human beings have created. Knowledge geared to performance and achievement, 'domination knowledge' as Max Sheler calls it, is acquired in order to dominate the world, to deal with the world, to come to terms with what we meet as already established historical development. This would also certainly be the approach of the classical theo-retician of political economy: Where lie the causes of inflation, of exchange-rate fluctuations? Why is the dollar up one day and down the next? Or, why does the monetary policy maker study the way money works and ask: How can we combat the international debt crisis. How can we use monetary policy to fight unemployment? So, in brief outline, these are the sorts of issues of concern for the person seeking knowledge geared to achievement, or domination knowledge, in relation to our theme.

The issue would be different for someone who seeks knowledge that serves an educational aim. This, very gen-erally speaking, is the field which previously comprised the majority of disciplines under the umbrella of philosophy. The most famous work ever written about money by a philoso-pher is *Philosophie des Geldes*, by Georg Simmel.[*] There he

---

[*] Georg Simmel: *Philosophie des Geldes*, Munich/Leipzig (1907) [*The Phil-osophy of Money*, Routledge (2004)].

explores whether money is predicated on our mental con-
stitution and social relations, on the logical structure of both
reality and our values; and, conversely, how money influ-
ences people's attitudes and the unfolding of their destinies.
From this angle, one has a very different view of the diverse
manifestations of money than one does from an economist's
perspective. We can ask what it meant for the history of
mankind when we first used a material as money: the famous
cowry shells of islanders, or *pecunia*, the word for money in
Latin – in other words cattle. From the Middle Ages to
modern times, we have used an actual substance as money.
And then begins this process of de-materialization, starting
with paper money; then the money you write – the cheque; or
today, in the age of plastic money, you push a card into some
hole in the wall. Georg Simmel described this process very
vividly. Of course, we can put the question the other way
round too: What effects are exerted by this sort of evolution of
an institution so crucial to our society?

From here we reach the third category defined by Scheler:
redemptive knowledge, or in other words the knowledge that
seeks ethical values, questioning norms and how they arise.
In relation to money this leads us to ask how the human soul
is harmed by this 'devil's invention', this capitalism which
glorifies money. Would it be better if we created something
else, if we abolished money? The fact that money plays a very
different role in the various economic systems of today is
quite telling. Consider the socialist economic systems: they
have money too, but it has an entirely different meaning.
There it has a secondary role, as a monitoring or supervisory
instrument. It is not the means of exchange, the unit of
measure and tool for value conservation we have in market

economies – but a supervision tool. So what we have there is a regulated economy in which, by means of coupons, directives and planning, society organizes what you as an individual are allowed to consume. That will do as a brief introduction.

WILLERT: I fear we must now approach the subject from a more metaphysical angle. Mr Beuys, could you now give us your view of money?

BEUYS: Yes, but not from a metaphysical angle. Many people know I've been involved with sculpture, that I'm a sculptor. Somewhat fewer, let's say 45 per cent of those who know I'm a sculptor, also know that I have been involved with social issues, for example that I became a founding member of the Green Party in Germany after instigating several organizations before that, such as the Organization for Direct Democracy through Referendum and the International Free University for Creativity and Interdisciplinary Research, and that I worked on an art concept which does not wish to have some niche existence at one remove from society, as written about in the 'culture' pages of newspapers – the so-called art world active in museums, galleries, fine art academies, the art market, the diverse viewpoints of traditional art historians. I was aware I did not live in a culture where spirit was paramount to people, as it was during the cultural periods of antiquity, such as in Egypt or ancient Greece. Instead I was conscious of living in a period when people are dependent – I say dependent! – on an activity in the whole context of civilization that we must call the economic life. So, as a creator of forms, I worked on a social concept of art, an *extended concept of art*, and in doing so tried to develop a consistently creative principle in such a way that it might enable people to grasp the core of society, the position of capital in this society. I developed this so everybody might see, eventually, that in order to escape this dead-end of private capitalism in the West, and centralized state communism in the East, the only way out is by starting from human creativity and from a real capacity for work.

If one does this, and reflects fully on such things, deepening one's thoughts to produce imaginative concepts of humanity's future, one finds that there is really nowhere else to start: we have to begin with the human capacity for work, with the famous concept of creativity – already bastardized by fashion of course – to understand that this is a concept of art in which all can participate, whereby *every human being must be an artist*. If we want to achieve a different society where the principle of money operates equitably, if we want to abolish the power money has developed over people historically, and position money in relationship to freedom, equality and fraternity – in other words develop a functional view of the interaction between the three great strata or spheres of social forces: the *spiritual life*, the *rights life*, and the *economic life* – then we must elaborate a concept of culture and a concept of art where every person must be an artist in this realm of *social sculpture* or *social art* or *social architecture* – never mind what terms you use. Once people have developed these imaginative concepts – which may come into focus a bit more this evening – having drawn them from their own thinking forces, their recognition and knowledge, but also their feelings and willpower – from the moment they have them, people will also understand that they really are the

sovereigns of a state-like whole, and that it is they who for-
mulate the economic laws which will allow money to be freed
from its present characteristics, from the power it exerts
because — and by saying this I'm already making a statement
about money — it has evolved in the economic context as part
of the economic life and is now a commodity. They will
recognize then that they can free money from being a commodity and that it must become a regulating factor in the
rights domain. People will increasingly see that money today
is a commodity, in other words an economic value — I'm
trying to say something tangible about money here — that it is
an economic value and that we have to reach a stage where it
must become a necessary potential, must act as a *rights
document**** for all the creative processes of human work …

WILLERT: The tendency then is not to abolish money, quite
the opposite. And I'd like to ask you Mr von Bethmann: you
don't think money should be abolished either. You only
consider that there is too much bad money in the world. How

---

* The precise meaning of this term is open to interpretation. In the further
course of the debate, the concept is elaborated as something that money
already partially does: an entitlement to goods or services. However, Beuys
seems to use it to signify a broader entitlement to human creativity and
dignity: a right to make full use of one's creative potential as both consumer
and producer. Later in the debate, Beuys states in clarification (page 32):
'Both sectors, production as well as consumption, must be regulated by
democracy which itself has to relate to money. If democracy is not related
to money, all the people's democratic efforts will be destroyed by the power
money can assume. So unless money has become a full rights document in
which the production sector and the consumption sector are embedded in
our society, it will continue to ensure the decline of human creativity, of the
human soul, of the power of human creation, and the life of nature!'
(Editor's note.)

much of the bad money should be eliminated? Do you believe – like Mr Beuys – that we could create a 'legal person' which could then also bring about this freedom? But first your opening statement, please.

BETHMANN: Yes, in fact I don't want money abolished. If you ask me how much bad money there is in the world, I will tell you that around 20 to 30 per cent of the money in existence today is worth nothing now and therefore should be got rid of. But following what I've so far heard here, especially from Mr Beuys, I'd like to express a personal *opinion* about money. I believe that money is a product of the human creativity which Mr Beuys has spoken of. It is a product of our civilization and our culture and it is even – allow me this comparison – a work of art.

BEUYS: I agree! Just so that, later, we don't have to say everything twice.

BETHMANN: Here we have a little patch of common ground, yes, but we'll soon part company. Ladies and gentlemen, I also believe I know a few things about money, rather than merely holding opinions about it. Which is what matters in my view. Many years ago, when I was still a banker but had already started to think about these things – bankers also reflect you know, even when they're still bankers, not just after they have stopped. I reflected on money because I felt that we didn't know enough about it. It seemed to me that money is one of the products of human civilization which has escaped from human grasp and which we no longer under-stand, like the magic broom in Goethe's 'Sorcerer's Apprentice'. As I searched for the real nature of money, I initially discovered an alarming number of answers, in literature, in science, but there was no precise answer, no real knowledge today of what money is. As you will remember, Mr Ehrlicher said money evolves. I wish to state firmly that we should discuss money only as *we today* are dealing with it. That is all I wish to speak about. So we know alarmingly little about money in the way it appears today, in the way it is handled. There are countless views and opinions, but no precise knowledge.

And then I discovered as well that most of these many answers and opinions are clearly wrong. It is not particularly worrying if you and I, ladies and gentlemen, do not know exactly what money is. But it is absolutely terrifying if even the specialists and those who are responsible for money don't know, don't *really* know what money is. If they don't know what money is they can't manage the money properly. That was my third discovery, that the specialists and those responsible for our money the world over proceed with their monetary policy from premises that are entirely wrong, and on a false basis, because they don't know enough about money. This is a reproach addressed to the specialists who deal with money, but one I can prove. Following this train of thought I discovered that we do have the capacity to know the real nature of money as it is used today, to know what distinguishes money from other things, from non-money, to express it in somewhat philosophical terms. There has to be a difference! And the result — I'll put it in a nutshell — is my theory of money, which can be summed up in a single sentence, which I'd ask you to chew on and take home to consider. We'll elaborate on it further this evening, as I will base a lot on it. For now I will only alert you to the fact that if you take this concept of money, this theory of money, and apply it to our reality, you will find the key to every economic phenomenon: inflation, excess debt, and the question of boom and bust. You will find the key to all things if you have the right approach to what money actually is.

Ladies and gentlemen, in today's modern monetary economy we must consider money to be every credit in existence in the economic sector which is expressed as money and formulated as a money value, which one participant in the economy claims from another such participant. Every claim or credit reflected in money is money, is potential money, is in principle money, irrespective of whether we normally treat such a claim, and use it, as money. Nor does it matter if any such claim is against a debtor so insolvent that this money is refused, like a cheque from someone who is bankrupt, as described in the article which I've brought with me. Irrespective of this, if we seriously want to make policies with money and policies for money, we must know that all open, unsettled claims or credits in existence in the economy must be considered as money. The consequences of this, ladies and gentlemen, I'll happily explain later.

Now I don't wish to carry on longer than previous speakers, and this is why I'll conclude for now with this formula. Should I repeat it? Every credit or claim in the economy with a monetary equivalent, expressed as money, and held by a creditor against a debtor — there are always two people — must be considered as money. From this fact flows everything which is essential to the preservation of our system, which is indeed also founded on money. Thank you.

WILLERT: Let us take a step back, despite the fact we already seem to have the key to the problem and could effectively end this evening here. Mr Binswanger, as someone who might be called an alternative economist, you have been particularly concerned with nature, in so far as nature supplies us with our raw materials. At the same time you have also arrived at the idea that defining nature is not something to be left solely to specialists; that others, ordinary citizens shall we say, have also found keys, however small, for gaining insight into nature. Could there, Mr Binswanger, be an analogy between the concept of money and nature, inasmuch as nature also changes depending on the way you approach it, on the way you think about it, and on what you wish to gain from it. In other words, that it is an open concept, just like money?

BINSWANGER: I would not see an analogy, but rather a contradiction between nature and money. First of all, I would like to mention a caricature which recently appeared in *Nebelspalter* ['Fog-Dispeller'], a satirical Swiss magazine, which shows a forest in which all the trees have died. In the forest stands a businessman with two briefcases, looking utterly appalled and puzzled, who says: 'What did we do wrong? We only earned honest money!' This drawing rightly suggests that there could be a relationship between money and the death of the forests. We debate endlessly whether SO_2 or NO_X or some other emission is responsible for the death of forests and other environmental problems. But here this cartoonist simply says that a deeper cause than NO_X or SO_2 may exist: this quest for money, in fact, which evidently does not have enough regard for nature. This view contrasts sharply with what professors of economics teach their students at university, with the perspective of classical economists which states, as the great economist John Stuart Mills himself once said: 'There is nothing less important or more meaningless than money'. As if it were nothing but the oil which lubricates the machinery and allows it to work, but not otherwise altering its operation.

However, a much older tradition in economics contradicts this classical perspective on money's irrelevance and meaninglessness. From the beginning this ascribed to money a decisive meaning, considering it a true innovation in the traditional natural economy, where exchanges were limited and done in kind. The monetary economy of the sort which developed later is very different. It is interesting to note however that from the very beginning of this monetary economy, while it was still in its seed phase, emerging and growing, that people already perceived the essence of this money process. This was when we invented coins, back in the 7th century BC: coins which were currency everywhere, which could be used everywhere, and were mostly used for sea trade when navigation developed between Greece and Asian trading cities, on the Black Sea, and so on. Then you had antiquity's *Seven Sages*, around 650. One of these seven sages, *Pittakos*, said what I think is the prime thing to be said about monetary economies. These seven sages were known for their laconic sayings. The Lacedemonians (Spartans) were famous for concise, pithy sayings. And *Pittakos* uttered one of these laconic phrases about monetary economies in three words, which in my view encapsulate the essence of modern economy right up to the present: 'Gain [that is, monetary gain] is insatiable.' This insatiable character of money where, like a snowball, gains turn into capital, producing new gains that turn into capital again, this snowball effect of money, was apparent to people from the earliest phase, and (with a few interruptions) has never ceased.

Today the problem is this principle of insatiability. The person who makes a profit is not insatiable, people are not insatiable; instead we have here something which is insatiable in itself, something which rolls over our heads – and as we roll along with it we reach the limits of our environment, of a world which happens not to be endless. I believe that we have here in effect a conflict between the principle of insatiability at work in money (we could examine this further but I won't do it now, we may come back to it later) and the finite character of the world, of the environment in which we live. I believe that this is the problem we must face and solve today.

WILLERT: Yes, now you've outlined two opposite principles, Mr Binswanger, the infinite character of money and the finite character of the world. There are other viewpoints according to which the world is infinite. I don't think we can go much deeper into all this. Now that we have introduced ourselves, in this second 'round' we could try to develop a few imaginative concepts. I'd like to ask the following: Mr Ehrlicher, could you picture yourself creating art, and you, Mr Beuys, could you picture yourself teaching economics to students in Freiburg, in Mr Ehrlicher's place?

BEUYS: Of course! Everything's clear now (laughter). Everything's clear now. We have already understood the concept! The decisive factor in revealing how the present system of money works, in the present political systems we are so fed up with, which confront each other, armed to their teeth — and how money will work in the future — is that every individual becomes a participant by developing awareness of his own sovereignty and by promoting right concepts about just laws of the economy which have to prevail in future. This is where I very clearly state that every human being is an artist creating new social forms. If every person is an artist in this realm of social sculpture, it follows naturally, surely, that Mr Ehrlicher can paint pictures and that I can occupy Mr Ehrlicher's chair. For starters! For starters! (*laughter, applause*) But then it is true that we must consider the individual's aptitude, shall we say, with which he or she creates (*laughter*).

Yes, all these things must be considered, that is clear. You can't just throw something out there in the world as mere assertion. We should discuss only the potential of each human being to shape social forms, to shape the future, to create the new social organism. Now, what is undisputed about this will of the people? What are the axioms we can't object to, that require no proof — the principles people see in front of them and want to attain through their will? First there is this very basic question of the future shape of society which preoccupies many people today. Maybe not all of them, but a lot of people know that the destruction or decline of the forests, and the crazy growth of our economy — which has gone so far that there is now a new party in Parliament called *the Greens* — means that in these contexts, culminating in the arms race between the two economic systems, the question of peace is on the table and has to be resolved. So the next question on our minds is this: how can we achieve this peace, or to put it more tangibly: how can all the planet's inhabitants cooperate economically for the benefit of all, without an iron curtain, without borders, without weapons or the destruction of natural resources?

The undisputed axioms boil down to the fact that people know things have to be resolved *democratically* and that human beings must be perceived and viewed as *free beings*, bearers of the impulse for freedom. People have to understand the role of freedom and democracy, meaning how freedom and democracy work together. This is the vantage point where they can see how the economies of capitalism and communism both fail. Yes, this is where they can develop such knowledge and act on it.

In doing so, people will have to develop imaginative concepts of the future shape of society – in the same way that the sculptor naturally has an imaginative concept of the shape of his sculpture. Their knowledge will organize itself in their consciousness and they will realize that money represents only one of the problems, though maybe one of the key problems of future social systems. They will experience the fact that, in their private destinies of course, money today plays a really huge role, because they totally depend on money. They are still often wage slaves! Marx said it clearly, and in this Marx was right! How do people expect to achieve all these things which a sense of freedom tells them are desirable: self-determination at work, equal rights and solidarity in the economy; in other words, a non-profiteering economy which works for the benefit of people and nature?

How do people expect to get to this level of awareness unless, shall we say, they engage with this social form and experience how very similar it is to the form of the human being? People's creativity likewise can't be reduced to a single principle, in the end only very vaguely definable, a mere

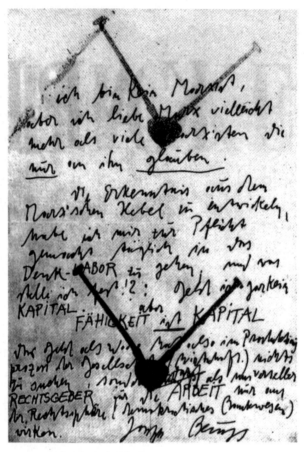

I am no Marxist but I probably love Marx more than many Marxists who only believe in him. I made it my duty to use the Marxist lever to develop insights: to enter the thinking LABORATORY on a daily basis; and what do I find? Money is not CAPITAL at all. CAPACITY is CAPITAL.

Money as commodity therefore has no place in society's production process (economy), but, solely from the rights sphere (democratic banking system), must/may work as a universal RIGHTS-GIVER for WORK. Joseph Beuys

(Contribution to the 'Luna-Luna' art fair by André Heller, Hamburg, summer 1987, large mounted photograph, approx 1.5 × 1 metres, text written December 1985.)

tautology that constantly reiterates: creativity, creativity, creativity ... But human nature, rather, is composed of multiple layers of this potential, these energies.

We have thinking, conceptual vision and feelings and will. Only when we have acquired, let's say, a certain picture of humanity, in other words when we have experienced humanity and observed it as anthropologists, one's own self as well as others, only then will this picture start working in the social body. We hope for a social organism shaped to our likeness, not an anti- or obverse image which would be a destructive image raising nothing but obstacles to people's evolution on this planet: first obstacles to the development of their faculties and then, also, threats to their health. But in the world we find two economic systems, one of which totally eliminates freedom, as happens in the Soviet Union and in communism, in the centralized economy, while the other, the one we have here, professes to be a democracy, but is in fact not realized, because every time a democratic process touches the true nerve of the transformation of society, power struggles underpinning money and the state spoil every attempt at authentic democracy ... In other words, we are dealing with two economic systems which are no longer adequate for people, and even less so for nature. The healthy natural foundations of humanity are being pulled out from under our feet, and this – I emphasize this because it's the heart of the problem – is caused by the prevailing theory and practice of capitalism – in our case, private capitalism. In other words, the power of money which prevents people from unfolding their capacities and realizing their aims has to end; the power of money has to be broken. But this doesn't mean that money should be abolished; it is the meaning of money as an economic commodity which has to be abolished. Because the real definition, as well as the answer to our question: 'What is money today?' is that money is an *economic value,* it is a commodity for sale. You can use it to speculate, to buy political parties – you can do everything with it, we have seen that already. To put it another way, it is possible to speculate with money, it is a *tradable commodity*, an economic value. Sometimes commodities are a reasonable economic value, when invested with real quality. But money in the economic sphere has no right to be a commodity! Now that it is a commodity, we have to break this character and transpose it into a democratic totality. Because money, in its essential nature – and here we are concerned with insight into the whole of society – is a *document of rights (applause).*

WILLERT: Mr Ehrlicher, I'd also like to ask you whether you could see yourself in the role of artist. Could you picture this? What role should art play, what kind of art would you produce and how much would you want to earn for it?

EHRLICHER: If I interpreted art as widely as Mr Beuys seems to interpret science, then I suppose I would also consider myself an artist *(applause).*

BEUYS: But you are one, for God's sake! As is everyone in the audience here! All this is clear already, we're already past this point! *(laughter and applause)*

EHRLICHER: Thank you very much, Mr Beuys, that's really very generous. However, I would not be so generous as to consider the statement you just made to be scientific.

BEUYS: That's another matter. I did not say that what I'm presenting here is science. I'm talking rather about the extended concept of art, about the creativity principle, about the creative being in every person!

EHRLICHER: One moment, it's my turn to speak now! You said you could take my place to teach in a university ...

BEUYS: Not could but should! *(laughter)*

EHRLICHER: That was the question asked by our chairman. And I believe we should stay with the questions we're being asked if we want to keep things concise. Here the question happens to be: What is the role of science? The role of science certainly can't be to preach world redemption.

WILLERT: Yet we were now discussing your role as an artist.

EHRLICHER: For this, as I said earlier, I would have had to learn this role of the artist. There my view differs from that of Mr Beuys. As it happens, I did not learn art, I learnt science, I studied economics. Now I wouldn't push too far with the question of what it is that science has to say about the shaping of society. I'll happily concede to the artist the high dose of subjectivity inherent in his approach to knowledge, but not that this approach allows for verification, for objective monitoring of the creative process. And just as he creates by shaping and sculpting, so one can say that a redeemer creates – the founder of a religion, the political genius who conceives new ways people could live together, better ways to live together. I would never suggest that I have access to absolute values which empower me to find, propose or preach statements about the best way for people to live together. This is why I think it is playing with concepts now to ask: What is an artist? What is a scientist? I believe these two forms of knowledge to be worlds apart. That has to be recognized, in my view. If we erase this difference, we erase things absolutely essential to our existence.

(Tape change)

... You can't impose certain values on others as being fine or not fine, good or bad. Regarding the way people live together, there are, and will always be, different views. I can't imagine we'll find absolute truth here because in all likelihood it doesn't exist, because people change and therefore the values to which they aspire change as well.

BEUYS: But that's a sad state of affairs ... *(applause)* ... if we had to resign ourselves to knowing that people are incapable of expressing their vision of society's future, with the two key axioms, universal and unobjectionable, that the principles of democracy, meaning equality, must exist for every human being (equal rights for all individuals) and that every individual has a right to freedom, as in self-determination ...

Let us proceed logically, starting from these two well-established axioms. Then we will observe that in the power of people's self-determination resides the strength which creates, from knowledge, what will determine new economic processes and also money – which for example is now wrongly understood as an economic value, a commodity ... I think I am the only one today to really describe money using a clear-cut concept. All the others avoid the question of what money is today. Of course I give my answer from my own point of view. Nobody has to believe what I say. But it remains nonetheless a finding that emerges from my laboratory, my studio. So I ask: Is this picture which results from my thinking true or false? I'm certainly not afraid of defining money with great precision based on my own perception, to say how it works at present and how it should in future.

EHRLICHER: Could you just tell us the difference between 'rights document' and 'economic value'? I don't understand this.

BEUYS: Well, you certainly know that today money is embedded in, let's simply say, in ...

EHRLICHER: Today it is not a rights document ...

BEUYS: Of course money is not a rights document in the full sense of the word, even if every individual with a banknote in his pocket naturally knows that this note *entitles* him to acquire goods for consumption. In the sphere of trade, needless to say, the money is already partly a rights document. All these things I say about money, I am absolutely not saying them to instigate a revolution tomorrow. I am simply saying them so that people can experience a set of concepts allowing them to learn and to know what money is, in its misguided role in relation to the regulation of rights involved in human work *per se*. So, in the economic sphere of trade, yes, money is a document of rights in the sphere of consumption. But now, I have a concept – again a concept – that compels me to continue characterizing the economy. Because the economic field has two opposite poles! It is split between a *production sector* on one side and a *consumption sector* on the other. Of course that is also self-evident to any economist who puts household budgets and production sites side by side and discusses the whole as an economic circuit. Yes, little by little we are approaching the necessary concepts! But money must enter into them in specific, tangible ways.

So here is what we have seen with money: the rights document operates only partially. But what is the credit system's rights position where large companies and corporations are concerned, in other words for the division of labour in the production sector? This question must be asked. Both sectors, production as well as consumption, must be regulated by democracy which itself has to relate to money. If democracy is not related to money, all the people's democratic efforts will be destroyed by the power money can assume. So unless money has become a full rights document in which the production sector and the consumption sector are embedded in our society, it will continue to ensure the decline of human creativity, of the human soul, of the power of human creation, and the life of nature!

WILLERT: We have now heard each of you describe your view of the future as it relates to money. Before things get out of hand amongst the panel, I would also like to give the other participants the freedom, or encouragement, to make themselves heard. So, a variety of views of the future have been outlined. What is yours, Mr von Bethmann?

BETHMANN: Really I would prefer we discuss the present

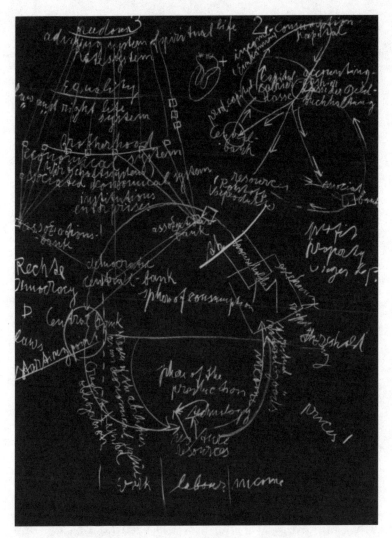

Joseph Beuys: 'The Capital Space 1970–1977', board drawing 2

rather than the future. If we understand the present, we will have a better grasp of the future. And secondly, we should know clearly if what we are exchanging are *opinions* about money or *knowledge* about money.

BEUYS: Of course we have to express knowledge about money, very precise knowledge with clear boundaries, knowledge which can be proven and verified through experience, checked by human thought! Of course! Did you notice how the supposed specialists always suggest I lack academic rigour (*laughter, applause*) because I'm meant to remain an artist in the old-fashioned sense of the word?

BETHMANN: Here is something else we share, Mr Beuys, the reproach of not being properly scientific. That's because we are very close to each other in the search for true knowledge about money.

BEUYS: And let's stay close!

BETHMANN: You will have noticed already, ladies and gentlemen, that Beuys and I are looking at the same issues. But I'll allow myself to observe that Mr Beuys has not yet reached a satisfactory conclusion because he is still stuck outside the subject, in opinions about money (*applause*).

His knowledge of the phenomenon of money, of the nature of money itself, is not precise. But that's what is necessary. Allow me to stress this difference repeatedly, before I also express two or three opinions about money. What we have heard until now has been nothing but opinions, voiced by all the participants except me (*laughter*). You have heard that money has a bad effect, that money is the essence of private capitalism, which by the way is true. Ladies and gentlemen, my opinion about money is that money is fully amoral, that money is neither good nor bad, that money therefore should be neither praised nor cursed, but that it should be managed properly and correctly to preserve the value it has for us, the people, to keep it reliable and a usable tool. Such is the task for us and for politicians. This can only be done through real knowledge – not opinion, knowledge – of what money is and how the mechanism of money works, how this organism operates; this we must know. If we don't know this we cannot have a proper monetary policy. And I say that ignorance about money is the root of all misery today. We are heading for very difficult economic developments. I am convinced of it, and the decisive factor in this is the failure to master the question of money. This is again a point of convergence with Mr Beuys. Mr Beuys says – once again only giving an opinion – that money is the essential element of private capitalism. Yes, I am convinced of that as well. But I don't conclude from this that money has to change, that money has to be redeemed from its wicked nature, has to be humanized. Money is just like everything else in civilization's evolution, a given human creation from the start. It's a product of the human spirit and the social context. Today's money is the result of a long history, and the issue is not about redeeming its devilish character, about cleansing it of its nasty effects, but about keeping it in good health, keeping it stable and reliable, usable as a tool. And for this reason I come to these opinions about money.

But l wish to ask: Do we only want to discuss opinions? – which is much more interesting and entertaining – or do we want to face this very sober, I think very scientific question (this in itself is a scientific question): What is money really, what is its real nature? I already gave my answer. Now I want to mention some two or three aspects or consequences derived from this formula defining money — 'Every claim or debt in existence . . .' and so on. This means, and here, above all, lies the key, ladies and gentlemen, that money (understood in this way) exists between us, in the economy, in the human community, in an independent process of creation between us. Whenever two people are in a debt relationship, whenever two economic partners, or also institutions, agree to new debts, then new money has appeared: money is created. The word 'creation' should really please Mr Beuys as well. Here it is similar to love: two people are required for love to exist in the world. For new money to exist, two are also required: a debtor and a creditor. We can take the analogy further, leading to another: money is not produced in some central factory, in some bank, and distributed in the economy and among the people — this is a completely false notion! Money in the modern economy appears every time a new economic claim arises.

BEUYS: I must say I am of a somewhat different opinion.

BETHMANN: Everybody can see the process for themselves, I can tell you very briefly: every purchase on account creates money; any statement of interest creates money. New money appears with every new debt, and money disappears from the world first when a debt is repaid — then the claim of the old creditor toward his debtor is void — and secondly, when creditors relinquish their claim. That is the other way money is destroyed, and it happens with every bankruptcy and every legal foreclosure. That's what I wanted to say now, in a scientifically exact and objective way, as knowledge about the laws of money.

BINSWANGER: May I put another view? Even if I admit that *today* debt is the source of money creation. Money is created by way of credits which are granted and then left in accounts at the bank, and may be redeemed as banknotes.

BETHMANN: This has nothing to do with credit, Mr Binswanger! When the Arab sheiks present an oil bill multiplied by ten and it is honoured, their holding in dollars is multiplied by millions in one move. That's a creation of money. By presenting their bill, the oil exporters create money. That's where it starts.

BINSWANGER: Well, you are going back to a very broad concept of money ...

BETHMANN: Indeed that's right, I am!

BINSWANGER: ... which exists already in Aristotle, who goes even further than you do when he says: money is everything which has economic value. This is the broadest possible definition. I may come back to this. What I meant to say is that new money comes to exist – as can be seen everywhere across the entire monetary system – not based on debt, but on the basis of two possibilities, namely that a substituting element is needed to realize a transaction. This is how transactions developed, with people saying: I have something which I want to sell; the other, who wants what I have, does not have what I want; therefore I accept some element as a substitute. It could be shells or something else. Then I can use this in the next phase of the process, when I have found what I need. This is one reason money came to exist, not consciously, but automatically, through the search for an intermediary element which would make transactions easier, help commerce. However, in this process one or two goods emerged which were perceived to have some intrinsic value, other than as intermediary materials, namely silver and gold. So silver and gold had value in and of themselves: they were desired because of this value and not just as intermediary elements. The fascination surrounding silver and gold plays an essential role in the emergence of a monetary economy.

This potential for the creation of money was then later developed when we said: we can put into circulation banknotes of all sorts which are then redeemable in silver and gold. However in the end there was not enough silver and gold, and finally, in 1931 – in London – the silver and gold currencies were abolished, most notably the gold standard. And what did we do instead? We said: the banknotes are a legal means of payment. Go forth and buy with them! But prices weren't defined. Effectively, prices are forever evolving, because of inflation, because we always create more money, put more banknotes into circulation. And this is how we lost the connection with what was tangible in money. To correct this loss, to make it more palatable, it is increasingly the case that one can earn interest on deposited money. Today, in the United States, interest is paid even on current accounts into which salaries are paid, because otherwise people wouldn't keep their money. They would prefer to spend it, which would in turn drive inflation higher.

Underlying this whole process we can see that money was an end in itself from an early stage, in the form of silver and gold. There is a book by Laum, called *Heiliges Geld*[*], which

---

[*] Bernhard Laum: *Heiliges Geld* ['Sacred Money'], Tübigen 1924.

explains how money emerges from what is sacred. This sacred character of money is still apparent today, having evolved into a means of generating interest (and no longer a metal, a precious metal, silver or gold). And I think that if we don't recognize this sacred aspect of money, we can't understand the present situation, this quest for money we have, also in today's banknotes whose substance is worthless but which are intrinsically desired nonetheless.

BEUYS: I must say that I also believe money is desired as an end in itself. But let us first get back to this story of debt, this issue of debt. I see it almost as a sort of mythology, what Mr von Bethmann is telling us here, with the debt complex whereby debt is seen as creating money. In reality – everyone knows this as well as I do – if for example I ask my wife, who keeps my accounts: 'Is there enough cash to do such and such a thing?', she'll say: 'Yes, there is. But you have to deduct half of it because it belongs to the tax office.' I didn't notice that the tax office, by taking something from me ...

BETHMANN: We hope you pay higher taxes, Mr Beuys!

BEUYS: Yes, well, just a minute! I pay a lot of taxes, for sure. So, the tax office taking that money from me would trigger a monetary process in my household that creates money ... (*laughter*) ... Well, it doesn't make sense to me.

BETHMANN: This requires two people, that is what I said.

BEUYS: Yes, yes, two. One is the tax office and the other one is me (*laughter*). That is so obvious it shouldn't have to be said!

Now, money is supposedly suppressed, or destroyed, the moment I give the tax office what they want, this is what Mr Bethmann is telling us. But the following month there is already another bill from the tax office. I must say I fail to see how, through these never-ending payments of debt ... Because these debts are defined by the law we have procured for ourselves, of our own choice shall we say, in this so called 'free and democratic order'. It never ends! Which is to say: I don't see any money being destroyed or any creative process with money related to this ceaseless repayment of debts. And everyone will have the same experience. No individual can see anything positive for himself arising from this whole process, no matter which way he looks at the problem! And that is because there simply is no way to explain how it is supposed to happen!

The other thing science can show about money is a view of its evolution through history; but that is of very little importance when it comes to the place of money today. Of course 'Geld' ['money'] comes from 'Gold', same etymology. But it comes equally from 'Geltung' ['validity'], meaning the value people fix based on their perception of a natural right. The word 'Geltung' is rooted in representations of a natural right, while the word 'Gold' is rooted in the economy of barter! Here's the real concept which has not been mentioned yet, and it should have been! Of course in ancient times people satisfied their needs through barter: a pig exchanged for a cart for example. This bartering economy is not possible in a highly developed industrial society. I can't very well step into the tram with a pig and tell the driver: here is a pig. How could he handle this? Slice himself a piece? So, with the bourgeois revolution and industrialization which later brought the radical division of labour, the economy evolved towards monetary exchange: that is precisely the shift to capitalism. One of the fathers of this economy, Adam Smith – another is Ricardo – truly developed this system of capitalism and showed how to consider these processes in terms of economic ideas. And there, money remains a means of exchange. So in the capitalist system money is still a means of exchange, a form of merchandise. We can argue as much as we want: it remains a commodity. And let's not forget that with the bourgeois revolution, or after the bourgeois revolution started, the workers, otherwise known as the proletariat, who felt themselves robbed of their share of the production process, said: we won't accept selling our creativity – meaning our work – through the salaried relationship, this violates human dignity! Yet today we are still in this situation unworthy of humanity! (*applause*). So, people's creativity is, shall we say, rewarded with a bit of merchandise and by something which should no longer exist in the economy! The result is, of course, the polarity between capital and labour, in other words: the emergence of the trade unions. This game unworthy of humanity, which we're witnessing today between trade unions – meaning those who defend labour – and those who, shall we say, as employers, buy this labour, this horse-trading about the size of the wage packet, has in fact taken us to the verge of catastrophe and this ultimately stops all creative work of any quality! Now we're slowly approaching the problem and beginning to see: why is this so? Why is money still at the stage where it can buy human dignity in the workplace, where it can simply buy creativity, where it can impose blackmail?

How is this possible?! It is possible because capitalism, meaning the economy based on trading money, is only *one*

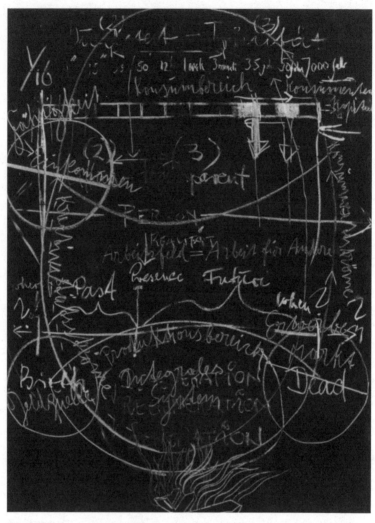

Joseph Beuys: 'The Capital Space 1970–1977, board drawing 28

stage in the development of money. But where the economy is based on the division of labour and production units, people – meaning the proletariat or working class or all of us, since in fact we all work and could all call ourselves proletarians –

demand justice of this money, they demand the democratization of money. This means that the individual who works and thinks a little about his work, this individual legitimately demands that the power of money as a type of blackmail exercised over human dignity within companies be broken and that money go through another metamorphosis of historical significance. He demands that money should not remain stuck in the age of Adam Smith and Ricardo's economy of monetary trade, meaning capitalism, but that the fact be taken into account that people developed their consciousness to become free and that, now independent, they want self-determination at work; so that we may finally consider the monetary system's next metamorphosis into *an economy of creative capacities*!

In the economy of capacities, economic forces can only be seen objectively as *two economic values,* comprising human *creativity* going to work every day, and what is born from this creativity: the *product.* These two things are true economic values. And they clearly describe the essential polarity of the economic system.

Money, still harmful now in the economy because it is possible to buy it and to speculate with it, and because of the polarization between employers and employees, must lose this status and shift into what it is essentially today in people's consciousness: *a regulator of rights for all creative processes.* In other words, overall, money has to express *rights* and *duties.* I say duties very consciously, because many people imagine that with the evolution of society we only have rights left! No, on the contrary: we have both. With the acquisition of new rights for everyone in the realm of work, new obligations also appear. So let's look at it in this context now.

EHRLICHER: Do we others have the right to speak as well?

BETHMANN: Once more these were nothing but opinions, Mr Beuys, opinions, nothing but opinions!

BEUYS: No, I don't call these opinions, they were, to begin with, a series of concepts whose absence of logic you will have to demonstrate!

BETHMANN: Which I can do, that is no problem.

EHRLICHER: It is quite easy to show the lack of logic in this story. How does exploitation relate to money? Was feudalism a less serious exploitation? Does the exploitation of people ... does the opposition between employer and employee start only with money? I believe that you have your own concept of money, where your rights document, which you see something like a purchase voucher, represents the right to something quite specific. That could certainly be a possibility, as we see in certain economic systems. But everything you have told us here is not in the least related to what we call money.

BEUYS: But that is precisely why the shite circumstances prevail that we have today!

EHRLICHER: You repeatedly assert – and so do you, Mr Bethmann – that we are discussing mere opinions. But in passing we should note that for a good hundred years now, economists have ceased debating what money actually is.

BETHMANN: Yes, regrettably.

BEUYS: Regrettably!!! We're eye to eye on that one! (*laughter, applause*)

EHRLICHER: I believe that sooner or later we have to agree on definitions. Of course we can continue to muddle everything haphazardly, so that one person speaks of money where the other speaks about wealth and the third about credit. It's a matter of conventions. But when science has developed the habit of working with certain definitions over five solid centuries, it is not very productive to blend these definitions together. And – forgive me for speaking like a professor – there has been no further debate in economics about the fact that money is the institution operating as the general means of exchange and as a unit of account as well as an instrument of value conservation. When the three coincide, then we have what we call money.

BETHMANN: But it's not enough to say this!

BEUYS: Indeed it's not enough! (*laughter*)

EHRLICHER: This is exactly the reason, Mr von Bethmann, that you are confusing things. You spoke earlier – I don't know to what extent the audience noticed – firstly about money and then about potential money. There is of course a huge difference between the two, and failure to see this means I'll be blind to all sorts of insights. For a proper debate, we have to have extremely precise definitions. Potential money and money are obviously very different. And your definition – every monetary debt or claim is money – won't get us very far. In fact, to acquire a twenty-year government bond you do have to pay out money ...

BETHMANN: In exchange! You exchange. The government bond is money, Mr Ehrlicher.

EHRLICHER: The government bond is not money because you cannot buy anything with it.

BETHMANN: Of course you can buy something, this is obvious! I can certainly buy a house and pay with government bonds, of course! That's what I meant by potential money. Even if it's not current practice today, you could pay with government bonds.

EHRLICHER: You couldn't ...

BINSWANGER: Here I have to support Mr Ehrlicher, you could not pay by this means.

EHRLICHER: Try buying something with a federal savings bond. The other party would have to purchase the bond from you; then you have money he doesn't spend, and he has the savings bond. In such a process ...

BETHMANN: Exchange, exchange ...!

EHRLICHER: This is the great difficulty, and this is our real problem: that new money can be generated from exchanges of this type, for example when a bank buys a promissory note long before it has exhausted its potential to generate money, and thus strengthens its profits. These are the problems we are wrestling with. But it's no good over-simplifying, making things so easy for ourselves as to say that every debt or claim is money.

BETHMANN: Yes, regrettably, it's a big mistake *not* to say so, Mr Ehrlicher. I've been raising my voice because the debate in academic circles, as you yourself pointed out, went to sleep, got lost somewhere. That's why I speak out. And we *must* get to grips with this.

BEUYS: That's why I speak out too.

EHRLICHER: The debate has not in the least fallen sleep ...

BETHMANN: Ended, you said, that's even worse!

WILLERT: Has ceased for the past 100 years!

EHRLICHER: Forgive me, but let's be precise. I have described what we are trying to define as money. And if I define something which I can always exchange, then the bond or securities paper doesn't meet this definition because I cannot always exchange it. Instead, I first have to find someone who will accept it. Then the next process begins which, of course, now becomes very complex: on what terms do you find someone? And you are in fact right when you say – for example about higher oil prices triggered by Arab states – that we should have been forced to renounce something else because of oil becoming more expensive. Because oil would be more expensive, there would be something else that we could not afford to buy. Were our monetary policy to have been set like this, there would be no new money. The problem is precisely: does a situation like this necessarily produce new money, or can monetary policy successfully prevent new money from being generated? New money should not be produced just because something has become more expensive and triggers redistribution.

The normal process would have led the OPEC countries to be in a position to buy, possibly, even more from us. They didn't want that, but we kept buying their oil. This of course generated more money, and a process of inflation started. This is the decisive thing: not to say: 'Every debt is money . . .' but to organize the monetary system precisely so that money is not created with every debt, so that the monetary order controls when new money is produced from debts, and so that money can hold its role as a means of exchange. This is why we try to define things so precisely.

As long as monetary policy is set so that money remains a means of exchange and a unit of accounting, monetary policy will be in order. This is why we insist on these concepts and consider that they don't need to be discussed anymore. But how to keep monetary policy in order, this is where other problems emerge. They are no longer problems of definition, but complex problems of cause and effect which we can only address if we stop arguing about this and that definition. The same confusion constantly appears when money and wealth are confused. Wealth is something I want to keep, something with which I'm not planning to buy at present. Instead I have accumulated it for later use. If I buy shares or bonds, I do so because I want wealth, not because I want money. If we also try to distinguish between these two categories, it's not in order to be overly academic but because, if we succeed in keeping them separate, we'll be able to distinguish their respective effects and we won't confuse everything.

BETHMANN: Precisely not, precisely not!

BEUYS: So, we just spoke about shares and bonds. Who amongst you has lots of shares and bonds? *(laughter)* So hang on a moment! Something else comes into play here. This social organism which calls itself a 'basic, free and democratic order' – in other countries as well, not just here – for many people then ... they can acquire ownership of means of production by buying shares. But the means of production in no way form a synthesis with money, nor with shares. No matter how we look at this, the people who buy bonds and shares and accumulate assets this way, they don't think of these shares independently from the idea of the power money provides! Thus the share, in my view, belongs to the concept of money. True, this money is stored as a share or a bond. This paper represents an ownership right, of a means of production for example, or another investment in any business; thus it is the ownership of a means of production.

Marx already said as well – not that I invariably defend Marx, but as powerful critic of capitalism he was right on this point – that through this ownership of a means of production, another buttress of power confronts the worker which prevents him from developing his capabilities, prevents his sovereign integrity coming to full expression within the overall state.

So Marx also dealt with this second point. I mentioned the first one earlier: this indignity of purchasing creativity at work through a wage. As a counter effect, this leads to the creation of trade unions to defend work. Of course they have understood nothing, otherwise they would be further along today and would be expressing the demands I have expressed. That is what the trade unions' demands should be! The demands I put forward should be the demands of the trade unions! But they have embraced capitalism to such an extent that they have become entrepreneurs themselves and ultimately are always the ones who help capitalism survive when it's plunged in crisis.

BETHMANN: How do you propose to pay for work if not with money?

BEUYS: Naturally, when someone enters a work relationship in a business, the business has the *obligation* to provide this person with an *income* for their work.

BETHMANN: In pigs or money?

BEUYS: As money of course! When a business is credited ...

BETHMANN: Money is the most social commodity imaginable ...

BEUYS: Yes! That's right ...

BETHMANN: Everyone acquires the same right with the same amount, with the same banknote.

BEUYS: No, not at all, absolutely not! Because those who have exchanged their wealth for shares and bonds, once they have a lot of those and have then become owners or part owners of a business, they naturally end up on the board of directors! And this board of directors stops all democratic evolution of the worker's base.

BETHMANN: Are you still talking about money?

that money is an unfair competitor with commodities. This is because, unlike commodities which are perishable, money not only keeps its value but continues to grow forever thanks to interest. Thus he understood that credit and the production of goods could never be balanced – by a central organ, an issuing bank for example – while a system of interest holds sway as it does. Because the stability of money in a political and economic system can never be secured unless there is a balance between the goods produced and the money created by the credit bank, as income for those who work, naturally. All money is originally credited as income to employees. And a business not only produces income, but also goods. This was Steiner's point of view. From which he naturally concluded that stable circulation of money – you could also say, balance in an economy, or, under certain circumstances, what the Greens mean when they speak of the ecological economic cycle – this stability is only secured once all money issued is matched by the goods produced, no more no less, and when in the process of buying these goods, in society's consumer sphere, this money loses its value.

(*Tape change*)

WILLERT: It is ten-thirty, and we would like to open up the debate to questions from the audience. We have just heard Mr Beuys tell us that the balance between money and values, meaning goods produced, may be out of kilter, and there I have to disagree with Mr Beuys. I would like to hand this question back to the panel.

Naturally – and in fact this is its great virtue – capitalism produces a constant balance between money and goods. It is

*P.S. I have been following the debate surrounding your ideas on
economics and find that, through dire intellectual approaches, your
opponents are unable to warm the ground of will, are therefore
prevented from feeling properly; and that this ultimately and inevitably
produces thoughts that have not passed through the fire – which is
something so necessary for thinking about money and the economic
system in particular.*

From a letter from Joseph Beuys to Wilhelm Schmundt, August 1976

true that the goods you can then buy are stocks or promissory
notes, or things initially costing no resources – and this is
why I speak of virtue! But next, these uses of money – let's say
as stocks – lead to a very precise future. All depends whether
I buy shares from an automobile manufacturer or an artist's
guild. They don't have the same project for the future: the car-
maker very naturally expects that in the year 2000 cars will
still be driving around, whereas the art producer may have
very different future plans or outlook ...

BEUYS: First a better car! All these shite cars fouling nature! (*applause and laughter*)

WILLERT: In any event, the balance is not affected. Goods are delivered against money but we must let go of the old notion of goods. We shouldn't call goods only something that has wheels or is edible; the concept of goods itself has become much larger.

BINSWANGER: I would like to propose that we open the debate here.

MEMBER OF AUDIENCE: Mr Bethmann has written a book about the history of interest and compound interest. I would have liked – others perhaps as well – to hear more details about the effects of this interest and compound interest on money. Because it seems to be a very big problem for the world economy.

BEUYS: There you go, Bethmann: 'The Interest Catastrophe'.

BETHMANN: We will shortly feel its effects. There has never been a proliferation of money at this level – a proliferation of bad money as we have seen in the past five or six years. And this essentially relates to the fact that we have never before in history had so long a period of such high interest rates, especially in the leading currencies. This is not an accident in the system but a fatal development we will all have to pay for. As I have said before, with these past years' explosion of money, 20 to 30 per cent of all money stocks, which I define so widely, all the debts, the debts owed by Argentina, Bolivia,

Peru, 20 to 30 per cent of all these debts have gone down the drain — because of high interest rates. The interest catastrophe is on its way.

BEUYS: That's certain! But to get back to ...

BETHMANN: But these are the things we should discuss, not opinions, like the demonization of money. There is no point arguing endlessly about what money really is. Ladies and gentlemen, it's not about whether you know exactly what money is, or whether I know what money is ... no, that is not what it is about, really not ...

BEUYS: But I say that is exactly what it is about!

BETHMANN: It is not about whether you know how your radio works, it is not about whether you know why the forests die. It is about whether the specialists know ... (*protests from the audience*) ... and those in positions of responsibility. And they don't even know!

BEUYS: Exactly!

BETHMANN: Today we know about the death of the forests, the specialists know more about the causes of this than they do about money, about the death of money; yet today we face the death of money. The specialists don't know what causes the death of money. This is the situation we have today. I am very glad this theme was brought up early, considering how relevant the comparison is.

BEUYS: True! What Mr von Bethmann says is true, money is

dency, private ownership of the means of production, and profit as the driving force! These concepts are responsible for making the whole of society sick and pushing humanity down into an abyss.

BETHMANN: Read my book, Mr Beuys, you will end up having other ideas! *(laughter, applause)*

BEUYS: I am willing to believe it! I even hope to have better ideas!

BETHMANN: Yes, better.

BEUYS: Yes, and this is why I say we still see eye to eye *(laughter)*.

EHRLICHER: I only want to stress that earlier Mr Beuys gave a fine description of the process by which money is created, as it really works today, not as he believes it should work. New money in fact really appears today in such a way that, when something is produced ... The Central Bank's monetary supply is covered today by three-month allowances. And after three months the money is always gone. Generally speaking it has disappeared even before the goods are consumed. This is really how the process of creating new money is set up, and it has been so for a very long time. The difficulties you are concerned with, what you criticize and gets you such applause, have in fact nothing to do with money. You yourself admit that you can't find something other than money to pay the worker. If you're suggesting the worker should no longer be a worker ...

BEUYS: No, not 'pay for work', that is not the right concept! I'm sorry! That is the wrong concept!

EHRLICHER: OK then. We are talking about money today, Mr Beuys. If you decide the worker is now an entrepreneur, he will earn a profit, you can call it what you want. I don't care. He will eventually receive money.

I believe that we have constantly been speaking about very different things. You want an entirely different system. You want to have someone granting credit according to ethical criteria. We can very well discuss that, but it is a very different system from the one we have now. We can certainly debate whether the system we have makes sense. But then you will have a system in which money as we understand it doesn't exist. So you could call this a need for money to undergo a metamorphosis ...

BEUYS: Right!

EHRLICHER: Then money would lose its character as a universal remittance, as a universal means of exchange, in fact what we consider in our economy to be the degree of freedom specific to money. In other words, if, through my work, I have acquired certain rights to the social product, I am free to exercise my right as I wish, I can buy whatever I wish with this money. Your view suggests the idea of a grand, wise authority who now decides what ought to be produced. It always works well, Mr Beuys, to take pornography as an example, the public loves it. Of course everybody yells: 'How disgusting!' But when you have to decide whether Mr Beuys has the right to produce art or if nothing later than the

Expressionists is allowed, or if one person should be entitled to exhibit rather than someone else, then we get to the real problems.

We mustn't, when we compare these systems, just contrast the polar extremes. If we have developed the monetary economy along with democracy, if we have defined money as circulating freely and the freedom to buy anything with it as the individual's freedom of choice within the whole structure of society, then we have here an extraordinarily essential element of a free economy. The opposite, as I could now sketch on a board, is precisely the economic order where the right to produce this or that is decided, as well as who gets this or that. Like the war economy, which some of you here have certainly experienced, where money was nothing but a piece of paper and the state issued decrees about everything. But how will you organize this system of which you obviously have some idea, when money has gone through this meta-morphosis, when it is no longer a free mandate, but bound to choices about what we are allowed to do with it?

BEUYS: What you have just said raises many questions of course. Still, one thing is sure: I myself support the idea that money should be a mandate — but more completely! — a document of rights, not just for the person who got paid today for his work, or for another who is perhaps better off socially, with other sources of income than his salary, or for others who own stocks and shares. I also support the freedom of the consumer.

At the beginning I spoke of the axioms for the future of our society. In and of themselves, they are irrevocably estab-lished! They are non-negotiable: *equality and freedom*. Both.

Meaning of course that I consider it desirable that people be free – and be left free – to do whatever they wish with the income they have earned through their services and their work. I don't intend to go back on that. I just want to take us a step further: I just want to say that for human consciousness the problem exists that the structure of the business or company where people work should likewise be free, whereas today it is not free at all. Part of it is already state-owned, while the other part is private! Neither definition, the private configuration of companies – meaning the way companies are configured in private business – or the nationalized configuration of companies, both of which we find combined in the so-called developed, industrialized nations – neither reflects what I call free enterprise. I call that a coercive economy! All of that should develop into a free form.

So I've been speaking of the form principle towards which, full of hope, people are now turning: hoping for an economic order to appear in the sphere of human work, in the human economy – because human labour is economics – an economic order which would get rid of divisions in the world, first and foremost ideological divisions, and the real and ongoing cold war; that would end abuses such as occurred in deals done with the oil sheiks during the economic crisis, ending them in order to move to worldwide cooperation through new financial relationships, truly social ones, that foster peace and cohesiveness and really social monetary conditions.

EHRLICHER: Mr Beuys, why are you so sure that this story of the sheiks and the rise in oil prices was such an unfair business? Could you not just as well take the view that the nasty capitalists exploited these poor developing countries for decades and that now at last a time has arrived when these countries, which for more than 50 years supplied oil free to the big corporations, are finally getting their dues? Because they are a few sheiks? Of course this gives the whole thing an unpleasant ...

BEUYS: Yes, you are right! The sheiks were much better than our capitalists! You are 100 per cent right! First these poor devils were mistreated, exploited as you said, by this capitalism which you still try to defend, and then these brothers – I am tempted to say: Thank God! – take revenge.

MEMBER OF THE AUDIENCE: Mr Beuys, in your system, are you allowing for the fact that people can be very different?

BEUYS: Yes, precisely!

MEMBER OF THE AUDIENCE: If you distribute revenues to people, the same will happen as happened in the period after currency reform: some will save, some will spend. That is a fundamentally human principle. But if some save, they become property owners. Then, everything you denounce under the word capitalism would start all over again. If you want to stop that, you fall into the coercive economy of Eastern Bloc socialism. In those countries people are forced to enjoy, quote unquote, socialist happiness. Please tell us how this system you are propounding could work!

BEUYS: Yes, of course I will. You have described something which doesn't apply, for example, to the credit system. You have described something which shouldn't belong, as I see it, with the views I developed about the adequate way free enterprises should receive credit. You're talking about something else: the system of savings and loan banks in the consumption sector, themselves subordinate to the central banking systems. These are banks that work together, in the sense of mutual aid, in the consumption sphere.

Of course, the money somebody saves is a benefit to the group. Every person who saves thereby shows that he or she doesn't want this or that thing, doesn't have to eat this or that! So that everybody who saves shows how he is helping properly plan the economy — we have not even discussed it but the planning is the most important part, it emerges from human insight and belongs to the cultural, spiritual life of humanity.

MEMBER OF THE AUDIENCE: Where do you get this idea about human insight?

BEUYS: If you give people the possibility ...

MEMBER OF THE AUDIENCE: But this is pure theory!

BEUYS: Yes, of course, this is obvious. People today are essentially selfish. But at the next phase of our social will, potentially innate in all of us — if let's just say we think of ourselves as Christians — we will act to promote better human community.

I come back to the point you raised. Every person putting money aside in the savings bank system, in the sphere of consumption, thereby proving he or she doesn't need a lot, tells the economic planner that it is not necessary to extract so much from nature. But today we proceed in the opposite way. Today it is not the consumer who dictates what the economy does. We pretend it is so, but the opposite is propagated on television. People are bombarded non-stop with Dash, Tide and Persil, with cable television, with everything they must have and buy! And *this* is what destroys nature!

Someone who truly saves doesn't become superior to someone who doesn't save, but he gives a good example to the non-saver! He gives a better example of how our human future may thrive. And he is a better indicator for the planning bodies of a future economy which, of course, has to be planned. But this doesn't mean a centrally-planned economy. Indeed I support the principle of free entrepreneurs, and not of a centralizing politburo. I don't support a planning apparatus in the old Soviet style but of enterprises in their free, creative form. We don't have them. We only have private economy enterprises and state enterprises. Neither of these principles works.

MEMBER OF THE AUDIENCE: So, before this evening gets boring ...

BEUYS: But it is not getting boring!

MEMBER OF THE AUDIENCE: No, but a few people left already and if we want to keep the others ... I just wanted to try something: I paid 500 pfennigs (pennies) for my ticket and I wanted to give each speaker another pfennig ...

BETHMANN: Salary!

MEMBER OF THE AUDIENCE: No, not salary, no, no ...

BINSWANGER: Income? Fees!

MEMBER OF THE AUDIENCE: No, I don't rate your performance so cheaply.

BEUYS: An acknowledgment fee!

LISTENER: No! (*applause*) It is not for your performance today as speakers; I expect something else for this penny: As an experiment I'd like each speaker to say in one sentence, or better, in one word, one metaphor, what this penny represents for him. (*applause*)

WILLERT: Nothing is for free, not even the penny, although I didn't get one.

EHRLICHER: It will be a very nice souvenir of this evening (*applause*).

BEUYS: Of course I have to give this penny an economic or academic meaning, because I am always asked to be scientific in my approach, whereas all the others can allow themselves to be totally non-scientific. So: I define this penny as *gift money* and thereby clearly show that gift money is the best money (*laughter, applause*). Money lent would be a little bit less appealing, but if he had said: I lend you this money, that would do also. Under certain circumstances, I could do something with it. If Mr von Bethmann still had his bank, I could deposit it there for example. But he doesn't have it anymore. But of course I would have to pay back this penny, without interest, since he didn't ask for interest. He would have granted me an interest-free loan. All this is to say that I do, in fact, attach great importance to describing things as they are.

BINSWANGER: Well, for me it is simply a good luck penny.

BETHMANN: Based on my *opinion*, it is freedom embodied. Based on my *knowledge*, it is a one-penny IOU redeemable by the German Federal Republic (*applause*).

WILLERT: Well, I don't believe we have resolved the question of money this evening. We have made a beginning ...

BEUYS: But I contend that what you say here is merely an assertion. Yes, we have not solved the question of money but I think we still elaborated some perspectives that can help resolve it. In my view, this would be a completely fruitless evening if we said, once more, that only sub-jective views arose here, or diverse points of view. For example, what appeared as Mr Binswanger's point of view on credit procurement for the protection of nature pre-supposes that we develop a crediting system for this in the first place. By developing a crediting system for this, which until now has not been developed, we would take a huge step towards a free economic order, one serving the community. And I believe a lot of things would then coincide much better with the concepts I have proposed than is the case today in our financing processes, in which credit is only granted for short- or medium-term gain, or when the transaction can at least be redeemed in the short or medium term.

In other words, the right form — which could make the sick forest a task and field of activity for people — would be a *foundation* system. It is too late now of course to speak about the concepts underlying a foundation. But one thing is certain: the foundation, by its very nature, is a *public benefit* economic system. And I imagine the form of the foundation to be the appropriate form for the whole social organism, for its production and its consumption (*applause*).

Afterword:
One can only understand what Joseph Beuys says by having already understood him: an overview of Joseph Beuys's concepts of money and capital

by Ulrich Rösch[*]

One can only understand what Joseph Beuys says by having already understood him. To gain a deep and thorough understanding of the work of Joseph Beuys, it is necessary to understand the worldview and experiences that inform his work. In his conversations and lectures, he described a world that is very real for him. His creativity stems from sources of inner, spiritual experience or, to put it differently, from a new spirituality. If a reader were to compare Beuys's assertions with ordinary ideas and knowledge he

---

[*] Ulrich Rösch was a Social Scientist Fellow at the Institute for Social Research and Development Studies in Achberg, Germany from 1971 to 1974, where Joseph Beuys also worked alongside Wilhelm Schmundt, Wilfried Heidt, Leif Holbaek-Hansen, Ota Sik and Eugen Löbl. His research focuses primarily on new economic forms and organizational development.

In 1976, he co-founded a Waldorf School in Wangen, Germany, where he served as a class teacher and principal. Since 1982, Ulrich has headed the business enterprise Textildesign, which produces environmentally friendly clothing made from biodynamic cotton grown in India. He has lectured at the 'Studiengang Soziale Skulptur' ['Social Sculpture Course'] and at several colleges and universities. Since 1999, Ulrich has served as the Coordinator for the Social Science Section at the Goetheanum in Dornach, Switzerland.

would merely shake his head in amazement. Through rigorous investigation of sensory experience, Beuys came to understand the existence of a world of supersensible, spiritual realities. For those contemporaries who cannot see or recognize such a world, it might appear as if what Beuys speaks about is non-existent.

However, in this regard Beuys finds himself in excellent company with many modern artists. The state of modern art is a testimony to the growing conflict between the human 'I' and the world as solely material reality. Beuys regards this given, visible world, which is considered the one true reality, as a transitory concept. In contrast Beuys acknowledges an enduring spiritual reality, and it is the work and presence of this eternal reality in modern art which is of interest to him, challenging us to experience the world as it really is rather than as it merely appears to be. Franz Marc expressed it thus: *'I have never had the desire, for example, to draw animals as I see them, but as they are.'* Goethe, the great writer, artist and natural scientist, was highly developed in this capacity. He studied visible phenomena long and intensively, until he experienced their inner essence. A comprehensive study of the plant world, continual observation of the sense-perceptible manifestations of plants, an ever new way of contemplating things from diverse starting points and visual angles, culminated in his concept of the *primal or archetypal plant*, a direct perception of the hidden reality from which the plant originates.

While Goethe had drawn a schematic representation of this entity, he was fully aware that concepts acquired by this means are not rigid, but instead continually undergo transformation and metamorphosis. Goethe describes his method precisely in a preface to his *Theory of Colours*:

> In reality, any attempt to express the inner nature of a thing is fruitless. What we perceive are effects, and a complete record of these effects ought to encompass this inner nature. We labour in vain to describe a person's character, but when we compile his actions, his deeds, a picture of his character will emerge. – Colours are the deeds of light, what it does and what it endures. In this sense we can expect them to tell us something about light.[*]

In this way, Goethe demonstrates that we should not focus directly on the concept of light, but instead regard it as the living entity manifesting in colors. Thus he sets the scientist the task of perceiving phenomena in such a way that the idea, the concept immanent in them, can be brought into existence in thinking. Put differently, ideas are expressed in their purest form in our thinking minds.

Rudolf Steiner, who was a student and editor of Goethe's scientific writings, asserts in his Goethean theory of knowledge:

> Lawful harmony, which rules the universe, manifests in human perception and insight. As a result, it is a human vocation to transpose into tangible reality the basic laws of the world which dominate all existence but would themselves never otherwise manifest.[†]

And in the introduction to Goethe's writing on natural

---

[*] Goethe: *Scientific Studies*, Suhrkamp Publishers, New York 1988, p. 158.
[†] R. Steiner: *Wahrheit und Wissenschaft*, Stuttgart 1961, p. 165.

science, he further illuminates this understanding: *'Becoming aware of the idea within reality is the true human communion.'*[*]

On this foundation Beuys based his work. If there is anything that we can contribute to solving the urgent social questions of our time, we must first be willing and able to direct our thinking to accurately perceive organic social processes and social forms. This is an indispensable prerequisite if we are to bring about positive social change in our times. Above and beyond this however, such cognitive understanding needs to be shared by a sufficiently large circle of people; and an artistic and creative process is necessary to encourage new, independent thinking that leads to social change.

This creative process can only be carried out in community, by an association of independent individuals, and not by any one individual alone. Here what Beuys called social sculpture can and must grow as a renewed, expanded artistic process. On this path we can perceive a healthy evolution from social science to social art, supplementing the scientist with the artist in us. Beuys's successors subscribe to this principle, which he significantly illustrated and embodied in his work in the 20th century.

Modern industry's polarization of production and consumption

Let us now turn our attention to the social organism. The investigation of any living organism is usually twofold, in that we examine both its processes and its form or structure.

---

[*] R. Steiner: *Goethean Science*, Mercury Press, New York 1988, p. 91.

When we study its form, we perceive that it is forever evolving and changing, though not always in a consistent manner. Its development often takes place in leaps and bounds. Such changes in form, such metamorphoses, occur in social organisms as well.

Perhaps the most powerful changes the social organism has experienced to date were in its transition from the production style of a domestic economy in the Middle Ages to modern industrial production. A social question emerged from this transition that has become one of the most incisive and important questions for mankind today. What has changed as a result of this transition? When we look at a workshop in the Middle Ages we see the foreman with his fellow workers and apprentices, working on a product within the framework of a domestic economy. Traditionally, this was not just a group of individuals working together but a real community: the 'extended family' of the workshop foreman. Most often, products were made to order, or goods would be made in manageable quantities and sold in the marketplace. There the product would be exchanged for other products, and eventually, for practical reasons, money emerged as a medium of exchange, a convenient placeholder for other products. The producers lived within a protected economic framework, a closed economic cycle consisting only of products.

Modern industrial society brings a totally different picture. With the onset of industrialization, we can shed light on the nature of modern economic activity from two main sources. On the one hand, it is driven by the skills, intelligence and creativity of individuals, and on the other, it has its basis in the transformation of nature through human labour. Thus there exists a polarity between mind or spirit, and body, in the creation of economic values. However, since the skills of an individual (his spiritual gifts) are always tied to his physical being, in today's economy he places himself entirely into economic life by selling his labour. Many of our present social problems are closely connected with this issue. The workforce has become a product to buy and sell, human labour a simple commodity. As such, alienation and disempowerment are prominent features of the modern workforce.

In addition, modern production caters primarily for large-scale undertakings and is not conducive to individuals or small groups. Factories, where hundreds or thousands of people gather every day, have become the nucleus of social life. Economic life is developing into a wholly interdependent *integrated system* (Eugen Löbl).

Thus, it becomes apparent that a contradiction, a polarity, is being built into the social organism. The starting point of all production is individual skill, which manifests as labour. However, today this labour is employed predominantly in large-scale production. This collectivism is simply a consequence of modern technology and the expectations and requirements of modern economic life.

On the other hand, the principle of *universal collaboration* requires the *consistent support of others*. In essence, in a society where there is total employment, individuals are completely interdependent, no longer producing anything for themselves. All production and labour is carried out on behalf of others who require the products in question. In this way, economic life based on the division of labour works towards collaboration, association, solidarity and fraternity.

This tendency of production exists in opposition to that of

consumption, for the requirements of an individual can only be assessed by the individual himself. Thus we can understand the requirements of total consumption as the combined summation of many individual personalities and needs.

And so it is that the processes of modern economic life have resulted in a polarized structure. The domain of consumption exists in polarity to that of production. In this polarity we find different types of value-creating factors: the intelligence and spirit which manage and direct work towards production, and nature which is transformed by labour into products of value for consumption. These economic values follow processes of creation and elimination, a value-creating movement followed by the devaluing process of consumption. This fact implies that there is an organic nature to the economic process, and thus purely mechanistic models and outlooks cannot do justice to the reality of the social organism.

The threefold social organism

In the economic sphere we deal exclusively with products and their values. All endeavours in this realm take on the character of a commodity, whether they are generated by material production or a cultural initiative. As such, only the result of the endeavour, the product, and not the work itself, should be evaluated as an economic activity. The outcome of this clearly, and here we are completely in agreement with Joseph Beuys, is that the entirety of entrepreneurship comprises both material production and cultural initiatives. Thus the economic sphere contrasts with the cultural sphere of society, which encompasses all individual human capacities and skills. Furthermore, we must extend our understanding of 'skills' to comprise not only individuals' intellectual and spiritual capacities, but every proficiency and competency, including the domain of manual labour. To realize coordinated production activity, the management of this activity must be allocated to the spiritual/cultural sphere.

> This is first of all, the domain of the spirit, in which human skills operate, skills which a person actually brings from other worlds down to earth, which lie in a person's own talent, which lie in what he can unfold from these talents, which embody completely individual qualities, and which blossom more intensively the more people's individuality can come to expression in society. Whether one wishes to be a materialist or any other thing, one should be able to say that what operates in this domain is brought by a person into this world from the time of his birth, and, from the physical proficiency of the manual labourer through to the highest expression and revelation of human inventiveness, is something which flourishes only through a person's individuality.[*]

Between these two spheres lies the third domain of the social organism, the rights sphere. In this sphere of rights, law and politics, lives a sense for human equality, and here human dignity and rights can be safeguarded:

> And this relationship comprises all relationships in which the single individual stands as one confronting other

---

[*] R. Steiner: *Die Kardinalfrage des Wirtschaftslebens*, Dornach 1962, p. 48.

individuals: not as an entrepreneur but as a person, having in this domain nothing to do with the skills one is born with or brought up to have, but only with what he is allowed to do in the social organism or what he may be obliged to do, his rights, which endow him with purely human significance in the social organism as a person amongst other people, irrespective of his skills and of his economic position.[*]

In modern society, money is used to mediate a wide range of economic needs, interests and rights, from land and labour to the right to purchase various goods and services. Today, our money, drawn from a central banking system, is no longer representative of real economic values. Beuys portrays this process of money creation very precisely as corroborated by public finance expert Professor Ehrlicher who states in the discussion (page 59): 'I only want to stress that earlier Mr Beuys gave a fine description of the process by which money is created, as it really works today, not as he believes it should work. Professor Ehrlicher hits the nail on the head here. The Goethean phenomenological method does not try to imagine a future society that will be exactly as one wishes it to be; instead, it aims to describe the deeper reality behind visible processes. Instead of fantasizing about a utopian future, it seeks to discover social laws which correspond to the reality of the world as it presently exists.

Generally, banking institutions lend newly-created money to an entrepreneur as business start-up capital. The entrepreneur will then direct people to engage in appropriate

---

[*] *Die Kardinalfrage des Wirtschaftslebens*, op. cit., p. 26.

aspects of production based on their specialized skills and work agreements. Wilhelm Schmundt made the following remarks in connection with the management of business start-up capital:

> This concerns a task of social shaping of the highest order. It asks the question: How do people find meaningful work within the production domain which corresponds to their initiatives and skills, so that both human and ecological needs are met to the greatest possible extent?[*]

This newly-created money is given as credit to the entrepreneur, who distributes it to his workers. Through this income the workers are obligated to utilize their various skills in the production of goods and services. For the worker, money is transformed into the right to purchase produced goods and services in the market. Since our economic life has developed into a closed system, the bank system should be responsible for making sure that all the generated money that has been brought into circulation eventually flows back — within a specified time frame — to the lending institution, the central bank. In this way money will eventually have come full circle.

These few observations show how, in the modern economy, money has metamorphosed into a mere *document of rights*. Wherever money acquires the character of a commodity or merchandise, it inevitably obstructs or even destroys social relationships:

> We need only recall the fact that money, by becoming a real object in economic transactions, deludes men as to its true

---

[*] W. Schmundt: *Zeitgemäße Wirtschaftsgesetze*, Achberg 1980, p. 25.

nature and by producing this imaginary effect at the same time exerts tyranny over them.[*]

The third sphere of society, the *rights sphere,* thus contains everything that doesn't have to do directly with human individuality or with the circulation of economic values. The rights sphere affects each human being in the same way. This is therefore the only sphere in which universally human attributes, human dignity itself, should prevail.

One can see from an unprejudiced study of the phenomena that the social organism has developed in modern times into *a threefold structure:* firstly the spiritual, cultural sphere, which has to do with people's skills and abilities and is bound to the expression of each individuality. An individual's capacities can only be recognized and judged by an individual consciousness. *Freedom* is the basis of this sphere: *'self-determination of every activity through recognition of what is needed.'*[†]

The economic sphere is the area of social initiatives. A producer creates goods or services and then a group of consumers judge the value of this provision. Rudolf Steiner refers to these relationships as associations. People work together to create economic values, which are always directed toward the needs of other human beings. Herein humanity realizes the principle of *fraternity and brotherhood.* Between these spheres we have a third sphere, the rights sphere. This is the sphere of agreement, obligation and entitlement. The principle of

---

[*] Rudolf Steiner: *The Social Future,* Anthroposophic Press, Spring Valley 1972, p. 38.
[†] W. Schmundt: *Erkenntnisübungen zur Dreigliederung des sozialen Organismus,* Achberg 1982, p. 44.

freedom also means we must grant freedom to every human being. Every human being is equally entitled to freedom and therefore the social principle we must work with in this sphere is *equality*.

Three key problems of industrial society

We have described the modern social organism and in particular the function of money, monetary processes, and the manner in which they work today. The monetary processes of today are controlled by thinking and concepts that do not correspond to a true picture of modern money. This leads to management practices which are far removed from the essential nature of economic life, and therefore spawn great social injustices and problems for modern society.

There are three false concepts that strongly influence our economy today. The first is *private property in the production sphere;* the second is *profit* as a driving force of the economy and the third is the concept of *paid labour*. These concepts are all derived from barter relationships originating in the Middle Ages, and completely absurd in a modern industrial society of skills and entrepreneurship – which calls for fraternity and association in economic life, along with reform of land, labour and capital.

It must be said, not from the point of view of any social reform ideology, but from a view of the real world and it's inherent, essential lawfulness, that each of the three fundamental concepts, in so far as they work within the production domain of the entrepreneur, impedes the free shaping of a social organism to such an extent as to almost render it impossible.[*]

Like land and property, a business's means of production are not consumable. In actuality, they should not be represented by money at any point; they should never be bought or sold. They should instead belong to the entire work system of the entrepreneur and his successors. The means of production exist thanks to the lending institution, the workforce and consumer base – the community as a whole. As such, private ownership should only exist in the domain of the consumer, where goods can be bought or exchanged, or perhaps in the domain of the small economy. Means of production however, in the domain of the entrepreneur, should not be private property nor owned by state, nor 'common property'. The concept of ownership makes no sense in this sphere of activity. Only a right to free use can be granted to the working community (or the entrepreneur). Means of production by themselves do not carry any economic value. Only when people work out of their own free initiative, using their expertise and skills, can they be productively utilized in the economic whole. Here a new concept of 'entrepreneur ownership' has to be created, which gives the entrepreneur capital or means of production for his new, creative initiative. However, it makes no sense to arbitrarily sell or inherit this means of production.

Thus the first false concept is private property in the production sphere. Here we need a new concept of business ownership. The entrepreneur has to be free to do what he sees

---

[*] Wilhelm Schmundt: *Der soziale Organismus in seiner Freiheitsgestalt*, Dornach 1977, p. 30.

fit within the framework and provisions of economic associations.

The second absurd concept is that of profit as the driving economic motivation. The income of an entrepreneur has no economic value due to the fact that it must now complete the monetary cycle. Income in excess of expenditure cannot in consequence constitute a right of disposal for any economic value. The achievement of a profit cannot be the economic purpose, as is practised in today's economy, influenced as it is by concepts derived from an old barter economy. The purpose of economic activity should be to create work conditions that maintain human dignity, with high-quality products requiring as little expenditure of work and resources as possible, and geared to the needs of the consumer. In place of material incentives, one's interest should be focused on the needs of other people.

The second false concept, therefore, is profit as a driving force of the economy. Just because an entrepreneur creates business surplus does give him/her the right to dictate its use. Making profit should not be the only aim of an enterprise. We need to replace the material incentive with an incentive that derives from an interest in serving humanity – meeting the needs of other human beings. This requires insight into the general context of social conditions around the world, encompassing every human being on earth.

The third false concept which likewise still stems from a barter economy is the concept of wage labour. The most important social conflicts and problems of industrialized society are linked to this. Karl Marx's assertion that labour should not be allowed to become a product arose from this idea of wage labour. This violates the dignity of modern human beings. In actuality, giving an income to the worker, and to the entrepreneur himself, is not an economic process at all but one of rights. The buying or exchanging of work stands in contradiction to a modern entrepreneurial economy.

The modern human being feels that his integrity is diminished by selling his skills. All workers should instead be guaranteed a fair income within the total social framework. The process of giving an income must be removed from economic life and placed in the legal or rights sphere. Every person has a right to income to enable him to live with dignity. Only when conditions ensuring a humane existence are taken care of, can a person make his/her skills available to his/her fellow human beings.

Thus if we transform our view on capital, a tremendous transformation could take place in the social realm. I would like to point out again that I am not interested in making suggestions about how to better organize the world. I have just tried to picture and describe the reality of existing social processes. We often address and debate these processes in modern society, but we do not always have the appropriate depth of understanding. Joseph Beuys had this understanding and deep insight. He was able to grasp these new concepts of capital and money and see how to use this understanding for social renewal. Once we succeed in inwardly experiencing such a radically transformed concept of capital, a comprehensive, educational movement could emerge to share this understanding with the wider public. Beuys has served as a great example of such efforts.

Hopefully in the future, a sufficiently large number of people will have understood these new insights and will want to work toward positive social change. Only then can our social relationships undergo healing. We cannot strive to produce utopian social conditions, but we can eliminate the host of disorders in our society so as to allow the social organism to develop in a healthy way in accordance with its true nature. All individuals who work to bring this into effect are partners, are co-shapers working to create a *social sculpture*.

*   *   *

Beuys's concept of money can be clearly understood, in outline, through his blackboard sketches (opposite and page 87). What strikes one most forcefully in these drawings is his depiction of the circulation of money, above which is written *'Check this again after five years!'*

The blackboard is divided by a horizontal line into the production side (*'Prod. Seite'*) and the consumption side (*'Kons.'*). This in itself signals an important polarity. On the production side, Beuys has written *'Capital = skills'*. People's skills form the capital of a national economy. As such, economic activity is restricted only by the limitations in people's skills. Money, when issued for useful production, can be created in an unrestricted manner. This process of creating money currently takes place in the *central banks* of all modern societies. Money issued for productive purposes by the independent initiative of central banks flows into business enterprises. From there, it is distributed to workers as income. At the bottom of the page Beuys remarks *'Separation of work and income.'* By this he means that the distribution of income is a fundamental process of rights and should by no means be dealt with as an economic process. Products can be

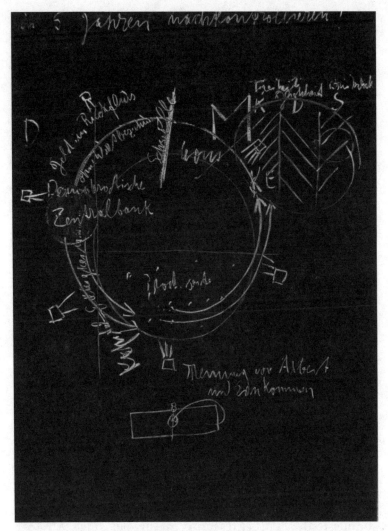

Joseph Beuys: 'The Capital Space 1970–1977', board drawing 4

assessed according to economic viewpoints. Work, however, belongs to the rights area, which invokes human dignity. The circuit is interrupted by a clearly marked *threshold (Schwelle)* (top/centre). This threshold indicates the *market (capital M)*.

Here the goods produced meet the consumer and money is exchanged. The consumer uses and eliminates the goods, or in other words they disappear from the economic circuit. The money used as payment flows back to the entrepreneur but it has lost all connection with the value of the goods. Beuys, therefore, writes '*Money in reflux without value connection*' (top left). Yet, today, this 'value-less' money is often used to represent claims to ownership of the means of production, sunk into land ownership, etc. Beuys makes it clear that this money has an accounting consequence but no real relationship with value. As a result, this has no link at all to legal rights. Macro-economic book-keeping ensures that the money in reflux flows back to the democratic central banks, at which point the money circuit closes.

The terms *Freedom, Equality and Fraternity* also appear on the blackboard. From the picture, we can conclude that the transformed concept of capital, and society based on inherent lawfulness, provide the foundation and impulses for what modern humanity can realize in the social domain. Whether this happens or not is to be verified every five years.

In the diagram '*Art = Capital*', one sees the money circuit in a broader context. Under this title, Beuys has drawn an arrow from art to economy and below another arrow which runs counter to the first, representing mutual dependence. Above this, he clarifies by writing '*Art – Shaping – Creativity = Work*'. This explains Beuys's concept of work. Work originates in people's creative potential. It becomes active in enterprises which transform nature into a consumable product.

An essential perspective contained in this diagram is that the democratic central bank is depicted as the heart (centre/

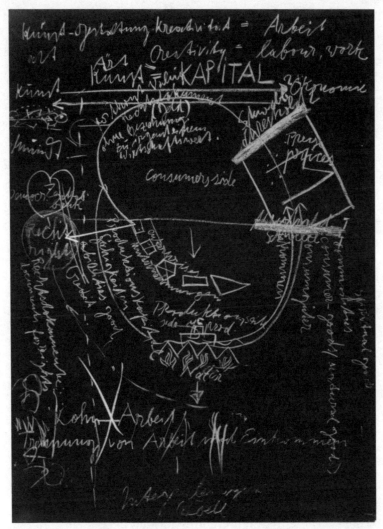

Joseph Beuys: 'The Capital Space 1970–1977', board drawing 18

left). Beuys links this with a new psychological perspective established in Goethean Science, which sees the heart as a harmonizing organ and by no means as a pump. The central bank is, therefore, not to be looked upon as a hierarchical organ that pumps money into the economy at its discretion, but as a regulating, monitoring one.

The movement of money and capital is determined by people's initiative. Next to 'Unternehmungen' (enterprises, centre), Beuys writes that it is people's *'skills'* which attract credit. This is also called *'production capital'*.

In this picture we can see both the production and consumption sides, marked by a horizontal line. *'Rechtsdokumente'* [rights documents] is written vertically on the lefthand side under Central Bank. Money is not an economic value anymore, instead it has become an element of rights life. On the production side, Beuys lists the various forms of enterprises, characterized by a geometric figure and below this *'nature'* in its many forms (lower centre). By working together collectively in production, people transform nature through their skills into consumer goods. 'Lohn-Arbeit' or wage labour is indicated by a bold 'X' (bottom left); this is the past. In today's world it is *'separation of work and income'*. One is activity in the economic domain and the other is a legal right.

Right at the bottom of the diagram, Beuys refers to the Czechoslovakian economist Eugen Loebl, who was the President of the National Bank of Bratislava for some time (in 1968) and whose research led him to the statement that the entire production side has today developed into an *integrated system*.

Consumer goods manufactured by enterprises flow into the market (right/top *'Schwelle'* [threshold] under capital 'M'). All the money which is given to the enterprise within a currency area must be taken into consideration when calculating the prices (*'Preise'*, top right) of a product. At the threshold of the market, all produced goods are taken into the economic circuit and money flows back to the enterprise. One now has to ensure that the money, as Beuys expresses it, returns *without connection to any economic value'* (centre/top) to the democratic central bank. Above the heart of the modern money cycle, Beuys has written the name of the Goethean scientist Wilhelm Schmundt whom he revered as *'our great teacher'*.

ALSO FROM CLAIRVIEW:

What is Art?
Joseph Beuys, Volker Harlan

'An intimate dialogue with Joseph Beuys, arguably the most important and radical artist of the late twentieth century, which takes us into the deeper motivations and understandings underlying 'social sculpture' and his expanded conception of art.'
— Shelley Sacks, Artist and Director of the Social Sculpture Research Unit, Oxford Brookes University

Joseph Beuys's work continues to influence and inspire practitioners and thinkers all over the world, in areas from organizational learning, direct democracy and new money forms to new art pedagogies and ecological art practices. Here, in dialogue with Volker Harlan — a close colleague, whose own work also revolves around understandings of substance and sacrament that are central to Beuys — the deeper motivations and insights underlying 'social sculpture', Beuys's expanded conception of art, are illuminated. His profound reflections, complemented with insightful essays by Volker Harlan, give a sense of the interconnectedness between all life forms, and the foundations of a path towards an ecologically sustainable future.

ISBN: 978 1 905570 07 2; £14.99